making love your priority

Kimaya

Making Love Your Priority
Copyright © 2017 by Kimaya

Library of Congress Control Number: 2017951366
ISBN-13: Paperback: 978-1-64045-877-2
          PDF: 978-1-64045-878-9
          ePub: 978-1-64045-879-6
          Kindle: 978-1-64045-880-2

Printed in the United States of America

PUBLISHING

LitFire LLC
1-800-511-9787
www.litfirepublishing.com
order@litfirepublishing.com

I could write about love my whole life through and perhaps that's what I'll do.

B ut for now this book of love, of knowledge, with my love I write to you.

W ithout any further ado I say to you,

"Turn the pages and open your heart and let the loving start ".

W ith Love,

K imaya

This is my wish to humanity wake up and remember now who and why you are here. Live the dream you hold so dear.

A life of perfect health, great peace, abundance of love and the perfect unity of all the above.

Can you allow yourself to be vulnerable? Will you let down your guard with the one you so adore? Knowing that you may be hurt once more.

Can you be so honest and true with yourself at the expense of all else?

Will you own your significance?

Be authentically You!

Stay true to yourself in every way possible, in all that you think say and do.

Will you allow your brilliance to now shine through?

In your darkest hours will you keep the faith and hold your light? Because in truth you know what's right.

Have you the discipline to journey within and the courage to share your discoveries?

Have you the wisdom to honour all that you are? To harvest such power and to use it always and only for the Highest Good for All?

Appreciate and reciprocate all things small and great?

Authentically You . . . let's celebrate-!

Love In Motion

*J*ust by noticing all the love in and around you moves you into the vibration of love.

*L*ove in motion, the sound of laughter or a smile to you from another, from you to another . . .

*L*ove in motion, that sunrise, that brand new day with its fresh untapped potential awaiting you. Is it that choir of birds breaking the morning silence with their songs of thanks and gratitude for the coming day's abundance? Behold, a new day's stories yet untold. Love in motion, grand and bold, gracious and quiet, young and old . . .

*I*s it love in motion this greater awareness, understanding that we are each a unique piece of this Divine and mighty whole? Unique and, yet, all oneness. The realization of this magnificent interconnection of which we are all a piece of.

Is love in motion that passion within you that drives you ever forward, opening your mind and heart to new and greater understandings?

Is it love in motion that one experiences from within as satisfaction? Fulfilment?

Is it love in motion that is endless and unlimited in all directions of time and space?

Is love in motion kind and sharing, patient, and caring with self and all others?

Is love in motion without conditions? Does it demand of itself or instead give of itself freely, unconditionally?

Then, is it love in motion that I experience with and through:

- My pets
- My family
- My friends
- My hobbies
- My contributions to my community and all other interests?
- Through all creativity and play and through all things that I Think, Do, & Say?

*I*s this love in motion all night long, as well as all day, after day, after day, after day? Without schedule, without delay?

*Y*es, it is then Hooray, to this unlimited, unfailing, ever-present love in motion! Yes! Hooray! I say, "Hooray!"

*I*s love in motion spontaneous, thoughtful, mindful, and aware of others? Is it open-minded and without prejudice, judgment or expectation? Indeed.

*L*ove in motion warms the heart, inspires the mind, and awakens the soul.

*I*s it this same love in motion that nurtures, comforts, and gently guides? From you it never hides its many faces, instead it patiently awaits your willingness to expand and grow.

*D*oes this same love grow and change through our life's choices and experiences, always without blame or shame?

*I*s it love in motion that we see in the eyes of others, in the freedom and beauty of watching all things at play?

*I*s this love content with itself, without limitation or discrimination . . . ?

Is it love in motion that speaks all languages—in various and unique fashions and ways?

Is it love in motion the heavenly scents of any number of nature's gifts, be it the flowers, or be it the fruits?

Is it love in motion the visual beauty encompassing the many forms of nature . . . ?

Is love in motion, in fact, abundant night and day in many forms, shapes, and ways . . . ?

Then, it is love in motion that express through songs, art, writings, be it work, be it play, be it night, be it day . . . Or in silence, that deep world of thought . . . where magnificent creations are born?

Is this same love equal between man and woman, whole and balanced male and female together . . . As one? Each understanding and appreciative of the others uniqueness, qualities and attributes? Together complimenting and completing one another?

Is it love in motion that has a deeper understanding and strong sense of knowing without question . . . ?

This same love comes in many flavours, shapes, and forms of expression be it personal or professional . . .

Is it love in motion that is fair and responsible, accepting and honest?

Is it this same love in motion that causes co-operation, consideration and compassion to occur among our races, sexes, and ages?

Balance in humanity helps to keep sanity . . .

Is it in Divine love consciousness that all solutions exist, however small or large the problem, within family's communities or countries . . . ?

Putting love into motion is the notion . . .

Making love your priority each and every day is the way. Choose to focus on the love in all things big and small — keep it up and this will be your normal state of being.

By being loving and seeing the love in others, this will help them to get there, too. Now that creates loving, fulfilled people and a world well worth being a part of.

Be open and explore, and remember there is always more . . .

. . . Open, Expand and Become . . .

Open your mind, expand your heart and allow yourself to become the unlimited expansive Being that you are, you are, you are.

Aim each day to be your highest love expression in all that you . . .

. . . *Think, Do & Say* . . .

Learn to allow for all that which is not yet known to you by being open to new possibilities. Many await you. Expand and evolve into the new greater You.

Dare not close yourself off from the All-ness that exists. Allow your discernment to guide you to this. Inside of you is an unlimited love beyond measure.

Have fun with this; remember, it's about the journey to the discovery of All That Is within every living thing.

Allow, expand, and become the greater of which you are . . .

Love In Motion . . .

*I*s about personal integrity, responsibility, autonomy?

- Self-Rule
- Self-Love . . .
- Self-Awareness . . .
- Self-Acceptance . . .
- Self-Perfection . . .

*A*s well as much much more than words cannot say; and, so it is so.

*S*elf-Actualization:

*B*e true to your authentic self in all that you think, say, and do.

*U*nconditional Love streams through you . . .

*H*ave you noticed yet that love is everywhere?

*T*he more you notice it in its many shapes and forms, the more it becomes your norm. That which you focus on you attract into your reality. As easy as one, two, three.

*L*earning to notice the good things you like in others; in sisters, in brothers, all family and friends alike. Learning to think thoughts that are based on love.

Choose thoughts of how I would like things to be.

- I am healthy and strong in every way.
- I feel good possibilities around my work, my home, my family, and friends.
- I am taking care of myself, really getting to know who I am.
- And making good choices as far as food, rest, play and work.
- I am making an effort to listen to my emotions – to my intuition.
- I am excited about discovering my hidden talents.
- I will take myself out of my comfy zone and try new things.
- I choose to live my life fully—moment by moment, day by day.
- I am unique by design, therefore, I am perfect being me.
- I am prepared to face my fears and when I add love these become opportunities.
- I am comfortable with myself and in the company of others.
- I choose to speak my truth with love.
- I share my gifts and talents with the world.
- I choose to be responsible for my life, that's why it's mine by design.
- I am learning to totally love all of me, just as I am is perfect.
- I totally love me and this love I now see in others.
- I am letting a little more love in everyday into my thoughts, my actions and all that I say.
- I am caring more, sharing more, and feeling at peace with this new me that I am becoming, what a relief.
- I am releasing the old and allowing the new, to myself I remain true.
- I am joyously abundant and wish this for all others.

Love is addictive and it lights your way, why on Earth would you delay?

Fill your cup and celebrate in all that you think, do, and say

Yes, love is everywhere, now my eyes see.

And this love I choose to be.

When we all choose love what a magnificent place our Earth will be . . .

Wa-hoo!

Bring it on . . .

Love

Let us take a look at what love is.

Is it just one thing or is it made up of many components?

How we each see, feel and act out our ideas of love is only to the degree that we have learnt. Our perceptions of love and what it is to be loved are constructed in our brains based on our experiences; these evolve as we grow in accordance with how we choose to react and respond to each experience. Everyone's experiences of growing up are unique to them, and so, too, are their perceptions or ideas of what love is and what it is to be loved. For example, some people may have learnt that love is when someone they care about is hurting them, causing them and others pain and suffering. When given a choice, love can be nurturing, patient, kind, caring, and gentle and so on . . . You then have the option to respond differently to situations than your usual learnt behaviour. Learn to observe what's taking place rather than to respond and react.

Observe your interactions with others throughout the day. Imagine you're the angel observing, and imagine how that angel would respond; this puts you in a loving and far more constructive view point that equals a more positive outcome. And it is fun.

To think differently helps you act differently and start to feel different. It only takes between three-to-five weeks to break old habits for good ones. A special note here: a slip up is okay, it happens. The good news is the moment that you realize you're doing it or that you just did it is when you have the power to confirm to yourself that you never need to make that mistake again. You feel it the moment it happens, because inside you it feels wrong.

Your conscious intellect can mislead you; in learning about yourself you must learn to trust your intuition, trust in the role of your inner creative faculties and abilities.

Quantum physics speaks of a unity consciousness, the unity of mind, body spirit/soul self, and emotional body. As you already know, you are much more than just a body. When you acknowledge and care for each piece that makes you a whole person, you are unifying consciously all these aspects of you. Mind, body, soul/spirit, emotion; these are where I believe your greatest potentials exist. The unity consciousness of mind, body, soul/spirit, and emotion will rocket you into a more evolved state of love, of wholeness.

"I am that I am," means that I now recognize I am mind, body, soul/spirit, and emotion with divine potential, as opposed to a body using a tiny piece of its mind potential.

"I am a piece of the whole, but not yet conscious of the fact," means I have not as yet unified with all the other aspects that make me whole.

Okay, the next wonderful revolution is in realizing that to feel love and loved for each of us this can be different. For example, as the mother in a family of four, she feels a sense of fulfilling love in the nurturing of her family through the cooking of lovely dinners and maintaining a clean home. Her husband feels and expresses his love that's best for him through one-on-one time together, and he makes sure that he creates this with each member of his family. The eldest child feels love through touch: plenty of hugs from his mum and touch rugby with his dad and friends where he can give and receive. The younger sister, though she loves entertaining the family by putting on shows where they sit and watch, she loves it best when they speak to her with praise when they acknowledge all the effort that she put into the show, even if it didn't really appeal to each of them. They still show her their appreciation through kind affirmations; this makes her feel very loved. Words of criticism can be very crushing for her, so they each comment on what they enjoyed the most about her act. It is not that difficult to notice at least one thing that they liked. By doing this, it has become their normal routine to notice the things around them and in others that they like.

Noticing and realizing all the different faces of love and the many places it can be found will help you to understand yourself and others a lot better. It is really exciting becoming aware of all the love that exists inside and outside of us. You choose.

Change, sometimes in disguise, is a beautiful thing.

It really is a beautiful world, and the more you notice this, the more it will be so.

No matter how much or how little love you received as a child, what matters today, right now, is how much and how willing you are to love yourself and to be loved by others. Learn to choose not to get lost in what was, but instead seize the power of what can now be and live it. Life with love is living at its best. All the rest falls away as into the love you grow . . .

The past is to learn from, not to live from

And, so it is now so.

Love is an ever-present, constant vibration moving in, through, and around us.

Everything in our universe vibrates.

Everything in our world vibrates.

Everything in our body vibrates.

Everything in our reality of experience is manifested in a vibration manner to us, in us, and through us and all vibration co-exists and mixes and mingles, as likes attract likes.

Okay, can we vibrate as one?

Could that vibration be a link between our spirit/soul self and our physical self?

I say through the vibration of love – yes, this is so.

Putting love into motion is the notion.

Making love your priority.

By learning to notice and focus on the ever-present love moving in, through and around you, moment by moment, you will expand into more of this love, this unlimited resource.

Dr. Masaru Emoto has beautifully captured the effects our thoughts have on changing the vibration that water holds. By photographing before and after shots of water crystals, he has discovered the responsive nature of water. Our bodies are approximately 70% to 90% water and by thinking, speaking, and acting with the intention of peace towards water can and will bring peace to our bodies and to the world.

Love is peace and joy, and everything that is exists because of love.

Love is our natural state of being and it is the absence of it that is the cause of all dis-ease and disharmony both within our bodies and our world.

So who has the solution?

You do.

Love is the notion.

Making love your priority . . .

Love Is the Notion

"Live your bliss. Let not one moment go amiss."

Your life is a symphony of *Unfolding,*

Ever-increasing,

Expanding,

All-encompassing LOVE

Realize this and release this into your reality. *Live your bliss.*

Let not one moment go amiss.

Deliberate, conscious, love-focused thought changes everything and anything, for this is the most powerful tool available to humanity, so use it and save your sanity.

As you read on, we will go into this in greater depth for your greater understanding.

Not only does love transcend all things, however great or small, in this process balance results inside as well as outside of yourself.

Remain light-hearted – lighten up – with whatever presents itself to you in your present reality.

Laughter is a beautiful form of love that heals and balances all, however great or small.

Laughter opens up the heart to a higher understanding, to greater clarity, also to the possibilities of total forgiveness when and where necessary.

Where laughter flows, love follows along with clarity, peace, joy, and creativity.

And, so it is so . . .

$\mathcal{A}$ loving heart self-sustains, always guiding us toward a greater or equal love vibration; always balancing the mind, body, soul, emotions.

$\mathcal{S}$ o love transcends all, therefore, the greater your capacity to Love and be Loved, the greater your capacity to transcend greater challenges.

$\mathcal{L}$ ive, love, and set free.

$\mathcal{L}$ ive with more love and become set free.

$\mathcal{T}$ o love is to live, therefore, the more we love, the more we live.

$\mathcal{P}$ utting love into motion is the notion; let these words now come alive for you in all that you . . .

. . . *Think, Do & Say* . . .

$\mathcal{T}$ his is where dreams come true.

$\mathcal{W}$ elcome to the inner you . . .

Choosing to actively focus your thoughts, moment by moment, only on the things that you want in your life rather than focusing on all the things that you're not liking or wanting.

Try this, start today.

"I am going to notice all the beauty in and around me, indoors and out."

"I am going to only notice the good points or good qualities in myself and others."

At the end of your day, recap by looking at all that you are grateful and happy for in your life; feel free to write it out or you may wish to paint, sing, and dance, whatever form of expression feels right for you at the time. This will put you into a creative flow that oozes love.

Keep this up and keep it up moment by moment day by day.

By doing this you are allowing love to flow into all the areas of your life and your physical body that, over time, may have become blocked or quite possibly shutdown.

Grow love consciously into every aspect of your life reality. By "grow love," I mean just as you grow your own vegetables and fruit for your greater physical well-being and benefit, you need to grow love to nourish your soul on a daily basis.

Can you imagine your spiritual well-being expanding as you allow love to flow and grow and grow?

Then, to you, I say, "Wait not another day, right this moment and all moments that follow sow Love, grow Love.

Let the love flow; love begets love.

And, so it is Love.

Let love drive your thoughts, deeds, and choice of action. Oh! Growing love is magnificent, no limits, no boundaries. Be WARNED: this can and, most likely, will become addictive and quite habit forming. You are fully responsible for the growth of your own love. No other can be held responsible for the tremendous consequences of your love growing; this will include great magnitudes of happiness, deep peace, great clarity, avalanches of abundance, brilliant unforeseen opportunities, followed by flash floods of fun, fun, fun!

You are the creator of your life experiences, therefore what are you waiting for?

TO LIVE IS TO LOVE, THEREFORE, TO LOVE IS TO TRULY LIVE.

To be living is to be loving.

So get loving and start living . . .

WHERE LOVE FLOWS, MIRACLES AND DREAMS OF GREAT CALIBER FOLLOW.

Choosing to consciously focus on love that exists in and around you in every moment will always align you with your greater truth, with your greatest possible outcome for each moment. (This love fills the voids of doubt, fear, guilt, anger, mental and spiritual suffering by revealing to you, can also be revealed through others mirroring back to you or via your own feelings any beliefs, ideas and ideals that are now in need of an upgrade.)

Yes, indeed, time to let go of all thoughts, outmoded beliefs, ideas that are holding you back from that all-powerful, infinite being that you truly are.

Remember, you are an infinite and divine Being here on Earth, having this Earth experience.

Awaken, live, love, and let be, in so you will set free your greatest potentials for all to see, share, and experience.

So, there are many dysfunctional people around you: at home, at work or both.

They maybe unbalanced, unhappy, some are needy, some controlling, deceptive, aggressive , dishonest or very conditioned which means that conditions around them, including your behaviour, must be just right or they lose it to some degree . . . so on, so on . . .

When you're feeling love, it transcends this and rebalances you. Inner peace and greater clarity are your proof. Yes, inner peace and clarity, followed with this sense of intuitive knowingness.; a consistent gentle loving guidance.

Tap into the flow, you will know as it feels great and the opposite is so when you're out of flow.

Open your mind and realize the potential.

Open your heart and release the many treasures.

This is the perfect partnership: an open mind and a loving heart.

The loving heart self-sustains, self-balances through gentle guidance, while the open mind creates limitless possibilities, as well as, activating your greater potential to be realized by you.

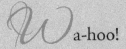a-hoo!

The beauty is that this manifests in all that you . . .

. . . *Think, Say & Do* . . .

Resulting in lots and lots of Wa-hoos!

LIFE IS A SYMPHONY OF UNFOLDING, EXPANDING, EVER-INCREASING, ALL-ENCOMPASSING LOVE.

Life is a symphony of unfolding, expanding, ever-increasing, and an all-encompassing Love. And, so it is so, therefore, I ask you . . .

How much do you love?

How much are you letting in and letting out?

Love in motion is the notion.

Making love your priority.

Love, happiness, joy, peace are our natural states of being. Your soul yearns for this return, for you to reconnect with this natural source of love that is, in truth, who you are, the larger non-physical aspect of yourself.

Love is the source of what we are, our true essence, and the more we choose to consciously tap into this unlimited love, the more we awaken and the more joy, peace, and abundance we experience in our lives.

Everything in life revolves around love, functions because of love, to the degree of which you are allowing or not, for this love to flow into and out of your moment by moment experiences.

Where love flows, hatred, greed, anger, jealousy, the need to control or take from others – all this goes. Fears dissolve into love.

Where there is love all those things do not exist. Can you imagine this?

No more wars, (learn from our past) no fighting; just peace, patience, tolerance, kindness, consideration, and compassion for one another, all co-existing abundantly.

With Love, Kimaya

*W*ell, the potential for this is now here and it all happens because you choose love.

*S*tarting with self-love. Heal yourself of all mistrust in your body, mind, emotions and soul; physical as well as all the non-physical parts that make you up. See yourself as the amazing unlimited being that you are.

*B*e gentle kind and nurturing with yourself, as well as all others.

*A*im each day to love a little more in all that you . . .

. . . Think, Do & Say . . .

*W*hat you seek, seeks you, stay true in all that you think, say, do . . . and remember, that you are so much more than just a physical body which you see, feel and experience through.

*I*nner health care, spiritually being aware.

*M*ake time each day, even if just in the smallest of ways.

Breathe slow, long, and deeply into your centre (your heart area) three times to the count of four at any time you're stressed or challenged, just breathe . . .

This will bring you back into your power instead of losing yourself to the outside drama occurring. You can choose whether or not you will participate. Next, remember to focus on the outcome you wish to achieve, for example: I see only the good and the truth in this, and the highest possible outcome for all involved. This is an evolved statement which opens the doors to a more evolved outcome as you intended for all involved.

Love with Integrity

Self-Responsibility

Self-Love

Self-Care

Take the reins of your life and make love your priority. How truly awesome is that statement, *Make love your priority?*

No other can be responsible for who you are or who you wish to become, that is why it is your life to be lived how you choose;

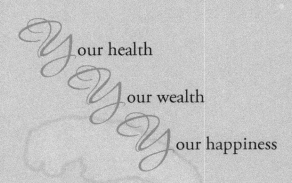

*Y*our health

*Y*our wealth

*Y*our happiness

*Y*our well-being is all your responsibility.

*R*emember always this: *your past experiences are to learn from, not to live from.*

*F*rom whatever you have come from, for you to live a life of love in bliss is within you and perfectly achievable by you. With focus, patience, practice and self-care; self-love will get you there.

*Y*ou will expand and become the Magnificent Being that you came here to be. Magnitudes of Magnificence await you now.

*W*hat will you choose to do with this information?

Will you . . . Ignore it?

Will you . . . explore it?

Are you ready to make some changes in your life?

Are you prepared to let go of outmoded habits, thoughts, beliefs, ideas, patterns, fears or illusions anything or anyone that may be holding you back in any way, shape or form?

In being true to yourself, honoring this truth, is a great gift indeed to all around you, at home, work, and play; be true in all that you . .

. . . Think, Do & Say . . .

Stand in your truth, what you feel will be very real. This will be your proof that indeed, you have made a wonderful choice that allows more love to flow and, therefore, grow in, through and around you. Allowing you to more freely BE the divine Being that you are. (Expand and become) Allow . . .

Be true. Release the outmoded. Upgrade and realize the new possibilities that now await for you to tap into.

Life is grand. Expand into your greatest potential, your greatest possibilities, moment by moment, day by day, sow love in all that you . . .

. . . *Think, Do & Say* . . .

*L*et this love flow – right this minute, right now, simply allow.

Be constructive and creative, honest and true.

Free yourself

To more fully be yourself.

*A*llow all the divine, non-physical parts of yourself through into the physical pieces of you. This will result in blissfulness, wonderment and amazement; All-encompassing, unconditional, unlimited love.

As above so below, from within, we will sow.

*T*his you already know, just to remind you, I wish to do. Now live this fully and be sure to play it forward, fully, in all that you . . .

. . . *Think, Do & Say* . . .

*T*o yourself and all others always remain true,

And this is love in motion, living giving contributing love. Or you choosing to consciously make love your priority.

SELF-REALIZATION:

Expressed through self-love, self-service or service of self, self-responsibility, self-integrity, and total honesty with yourself.

Within the integrity of self-love is:

- SELF-CONSCIOUSNESS
- SELF-AWARENESS
- SELF-ACCEPTANCE
- SELF-PERFECTION
- SELF-MASTERY
- SELF-RESPONSIBILITY

Until you are living your bliss, let not one moment go amiss.

All the wisdom from the many lessons of your many pasts are all that remain with you. As you expand, moment by moment, day by day, into the greater of what you truly are, allowing your greatest potentials to be made manifest.

So how about a little recap thus far?

Unconditional self-love would mean that I now accept that everyone makes mistakes, large and small; I choose to learn from them all, to remember the lesson or lessons involved. If need be correct the mistake, remembering that correction is appropriate and punishment is not necessary.

I can forgive myself and others where my forgiveness is necessary, in so freeing myself to move forward.

Expand and grow, this you know.

Say this to yourself and truly believe it as you speak it:

"Allowing more love into my daily life means that I will be exchanging pain for greater self-peace and perfection."

"I now exchange all pain in my life into gain in my life; I am at peace with my life."

LOVE IN PROGRESS; WHAT AN AWESOME PROCESS.

Remember, that choosing to come from a more loving thought or space, puts solutions into place for you to lovingly follow through with. Trust and allow this process and you will soon enough see and feel the progress.

Be patient and gentle with yourself. If you should ever experience a slipping back into an old habit, acknowledge the experience and enforce to self that this need not ever happen again, as you now have a greater understanding of the situation. Understand that the human brain will now gain a new perspective bringing you to this more evolved understanding. Open a greater consciousness that exits beyond the mundane level. (Pure non-physical love consciousness, accessible to us through us choosing). Come into your heart space on your inhale; allow yourself to expand into this love. On the exhale, outbreath, release all stress. This simple step will reap great rewards as you get into a routine of doing this with all situations in and around you.

FEAR NOT

For those who choose to live with drama or fear, this closes the heart and clouds the mind. So, then to you I say, "Why not have the excitement without the drama?"

When you choose and learn to tap into the love source within you (you can start right this minute by consciously breathing with your imagination into your heart): in with love, and out with any fear or excess stress. Three slow, deep breaths; this immediately centres your energy and as you keep this up, it will calm you. A great rescue remedy.

Should you choose to set aside time each day, even as little as five minutes, it will benefit you. The longer you do this, the better the benefits.

When you make the time to enter this still, silent, yet potently powerful inner world, you will be connecting into the greater aspects that make you up – by this I mean the non-physical aspects of yourself. This has far more significance, is far more vital than the limitations of the mundane world. Imagine if we were operating with say, even 50% of our brain ability; could this mean we would be accessing and operating from the greater plane of who we really are, drawing from the non-physical into the physical?

Talk about love is the notion and love in motion.

(By focusing on the love in our hearts and expanding, allowing this love more and more day by day into our every thought, deed and action, imagine with me for this moment, of this love with your intention and care. It will expand into a greater, more divine love aspect of you which, in turn, activates and awakens, bit by bit, aspects of the brain that have, until such a time, been dormant).

We are so very much more than physical beings. The non-physical aspects of us make up the greater of us. Investing time on this is indeed vital to us. Best of all, is that it is fun to explore, easy to access, free of charge; options are limitless as to how far you choose to go with this.

WARNING: *this is addictive, extremely fulfilling. You are very likely to experience great joy and happiness, fits of laughter followed by deep peacefulness and new profound calm. Side effects are unforeseen abundances in all areas of your life.*

Yes, this is so. As you already know, you are a limitless Being, having your Earthly experience, doing the best you know how with what you know at each given moment in time.

I would just like you to know that you now have access to the greater non-physical, spirit/soul parts of you, the parts responsible for creating your Heaven on Earth.

*E*asy, simple, and true.

*K*eep it simple, people. You see it truly does not need to be complicated. Get used to simplicity.

*S*implicity is the key, the answer. As always, you choose.

*M*ake your intentions clear; keep it simple and to-the-point. No need to complicate matters. Always, you will find that it's the simple things in life that matter.

*T*his rings true in times of strife. As always, you will find the little things, the simple things were what meant the most to you. Just to name a few:

- An unexpected thank you!
- Flowers gifted to you
- That welcomed phone call to you from a friend
- Money repaid to you
- Food on the table

- That kind thought or deed from you to another, to you from another
- Kind words spoken with sincerity
- Beautiful music
- Technology for all its comforts and convenience, lightening the work load
- A hug
- A walk in the park
- Exchanging words or sharing feelings/dreams with that true, honest friend
- Knowing that you are never, ever alone
- And, that no matter what, you are loved unconditionally.

It turns out to be, the simple things are the only things that really count to you and to me.

That magnificent feeling you have when you are making or creating.

I am soooo grateful for this . . . Bliss . . .

All through making love my priority.

Making Love Your Priority

By now you will understand the positive impact you will have on those around you and on the world around you just by effectively living with more love.

Integrity, Morals, Values and Principles, Update and Upgrade.

Treating others how you like to be treated: equally, with courtesy, consideration, respect, patience, and kindness too. Realize that each and every person's work is as equally important, that we all need, to some degree, to feel loved and be of some importance, to feel appreciated. Watch what happens as you express this to all those around you. Watch and feel the power as this draws talents out from hiding.

Kind thoughts, kind deeds, consideration, appreciation – activate your senses into gear along with emotions as you expand into higher states of love. You will recognise this by a sense of fulfilment, joy, along with this greater inner peace.

Appreciate – Reciprocate all things small and great.

This is a magnificent habit to be in . . .
Notice the good in all people, in all things.
You might even say to yourself, "I am in the habit of feeling and noticing love in all things."
Next know thy self, honour and respect, learn to accept. This means your flaws, as well as your strengths. Once you see where you are, you may aim at where you wish to be. This is a very beautiful thing, getting to know thy self in all of your entirety—totality, a wonderful life changing, expansive experience which is both rewarding and fulfilling. Getting to know and understand and learn to accept any weakness helps to empower who you are. Through self-awareness, you empower the person that you are and can then choose better, more loving choices, words and thoughts to achieve better self-balance. Empowerment through self-improvement.

Self-love, self-awareness, self–balance.

Balanced living means to live with balance of all aspects of yourself.

When you live in harmony with yourself, this has positive impact on your environment and your community, not to mention all those around you and close to you such as family and friends at work and at home. In fact, the better your state of harmony with yourself, the more you will come into harmony with your environment and community. *Unity in your community.*

Physical exercise, mind awareness as well as exercise (learning new things expands the brain and along with it your life), good mental hygiene means to eliminate excess stress or worry that can accumulate on a daily basis, depending on you, your work, your attitude, as well as personality. Upgrade and update your beliefs.

Making love your priority will soon keep all stress and worry in check.

For those of you that do not already know this, a happy mind means a happy and meaningful life.

(Emotional health, time-out for self with self, learning to notice how you feel and how to tune those feelings to feel good things).

To emotionalize means to experience on an emotional level or putting it on a feeling level. Expressing with feeling creates change on a subconscious level; the more emotion and feeling, generally the quicker the manifestation of the dream, idea or thought – you feel it into manifestation. This then, is a very powerful, life changing tool. The subconscious mind cannot tell the difference between what you're imagining and what you're actually experiencing; therefore, you can dream, imagine or feel anything you give enough focus to into your reality – into your daily life experience.

This will rewire the brain's perception of life which is based on each individual's past experiences. For example, noticing that you seem to have experienced a lot of lack in your life, try to now see yourself (abundant). You can dream it and imagine how it feels to be abundant. This begins the process of letting go of any beliefs that may have held you in the experience of lack. Upgrade to abundance.

This is a process; allow time for progression. You have to be willing to explore your mind, emotions, body, and soul at a whole new level.

We are each unique, with unique challenges, issues or blocks. Be prepared to find your unique answer on whatsoever level it may be on – sometimes more than one. Go slow and stay focused on the desired, wholesome result, remembering that life is an ongoing process. Keep it loving, and you're set to progress.

Live, Love, Learn, and Grow.

Soul/Spirit health; communicate and connect to this great loving power source within by simply taking three slow, deep breaths. Follow each breath in. This silence and stillness allows for the soul energy to pour through into your every cell, filling your whole being, mental, physical and emotional reality. Anytime, anywhere, these short-focused intervals of slow focused, deep, breaths are especially effective when in a stressful situation. Just stop and breathe, consciously following in each breath. This is your rescue remedy. On the other hand, if you have been still for long periods, for example at work, then it will benefit you greatly to get up and move about, stretch, walk, however short. This will activate your spirit, which well may have fallen asleep while the mind alone was busy at work for you.

The purpose in consciously unifying all these aspects – mind and emotion with body and soul – is strength in unity—makes each moment flow with ease and grace and with greater creative flow, resulting in a whole and fulfilling experience from moment to moment. You will be utilizing more of your possibilities and potentials with far less effort. Strength of unity – remember this and remember to apply this. It takes only a little conscious effort on your part and the benefits are instant. Such peace, such clarity.

Just as a physical workout uses many muscles, as opposed to one or two, benefiting the whole body and mind. Activating many to work together creates greater strength through unity.

(Stick at it) *Consistency builds certainty.*

The food we choose to eat has an effect on how we look and how good we feel, or not. If we imagine our thoughts are like food, the choices we make and the actions we choose or not to take make a difference to our mind and body.

Patience is a virtue.

Be patient with yourself. Allow time to integrate the new into your life.

Life is a process of growth through change and integration.

Those that choose to resist change will sooner or later find themselves changing anyway; and this change will not be as gentle as it would have been if it had been through your personal will or choice to make or accept change.

This is the way of life on Earth. We are here to make choices, to learn from these life choices and experiences and to grow from the outcome of these choices.

With Love, Kimaya

Do you welcome and embrace change or reject and resist change?

Are you prepared to make subtle changes on a daily basis; to make the effort and put this time into yourself?

You decide how much time and effort that you will or will not put into yourself.

You are the key – unlock and behold, with eyes that see.

Unless you close yourself off from all the magical opportunities that living life has to offer, your whole life will be an on-going process of integration and upgrading. Translation: expand and become the whole and magnificent Being that you really, in truth, are.

Live the life that you came here to live.

You're not just a Body,

    Soul/Spirit,

    Emotional body.

    You are all this and more.

Unity is the key. Unify each and every aspect of self and enjoy the process. This means to consciously be aware and take responsibility for how in or out of balance you are. *Fun—filled focus.*

Explore, allow, discern, and integrate.
Everything is wonderful—when you believe.
Live the way that you believe life should be.

Balance in all things in life.

Stick-ability, flexibility, spontaneity, durability, dream ability, imagination, and goal setting ability or simply allowing self the freedom to dream.

Passion, desire, ambition and drive balanced with rest, relaxation, creativity, laughter, fun, play and the perfect unity of these well-balanced aspects of yourself equals *magnitudes of magnificence.*

This is all about love and communicating with yourself and others.

How well do you Love yourself?

And how well are you able to communicate this love to self and others?

Unity is a fundamental truth of quantum physics, all One, or unique expressions of the all Oneness. It's individual and unique for each of us, while uniquely interconnected.

This means that each choice we make and action we take will have an effect on, not only our own lives, but also all other life around us. This is always so, a constant that you know—in one way or another, whether or not you are aware of this . . .

Therefore, the more you learn to love and understand yourself, the greater your love impact will be on all life around you.

Integrity of self, love with integrity, with this comes the realization that no matter what is happening in your life, you choose how this will impact on your life, on your well-being.

Simply by choosing more loving thoughts around any situation, love indwells and enfolds you. Resulting in a better balanced well-being.

And next because you keep your focus on the love in your heart instead of focusing on dramas taking place outside of yourself, you will be holding a more loving vibration in thought. This will give you clarity, as well as a possible solution that you otherwise would not have seen or being ware of.

Through love all things are possible.

Make love your priority.

The more love you choose, the less there is to lose.

So the more love you choose to let in every moment of your every day, the more peace and joy along with the necessary patience to integrate and appreciate this new found love into your reality, resulting in a greater state of being.

Make time to stop and smell the roses. It's all the little things in life that make the biggest difference in your life.

Learn to just be without having or needing to do anything.

You cannot do without being, yet you can be without doing.

In fact, when you're not actively doing physical things, you are closest to your true whole self, the unlimited Being aspect of yourself. Think about that . . .

Have you ever pondered the possibility of the 70 to 75% of the human brain that sits dormant holding a space in our heads?

What might be the possibilities of this large portion of inactive tissue with electrical pulses running through it?

Imagine if moving into higher states of love vibration (remembering that everything about us and our reality is a vibration and every thought that we think effects how high or low our vibration will be.) So, imagine if holding higher love vibration states or thoughts activate parts of the brain lying dormant that lower vibrations of love could not stir into motion.

Wow! What possibilities could be waiting for each of us willing to be, and consciously work at being our highest love vibration?

What is the next stage of human evolution?

(A very individual and unique experience depending on how evolved each individual's love vibration is. And yet that eternal knowing that, All is One and One is All.)

The language of universal love: All life interconnects.

And so it is so . . .

This we all know, as it is written in our hearts and remembered through love.

For every action there is an equal or opposite reaction. The higher the love, the greater the reaction of this love will be. Of course, the reverse of this is so, through our history this we know.

Our ancestors knew this and lived as one with Earth and with the true knowledge of our origins. They lived love in its higher states, in every way, until came the day that they allowed themselves to be distorted by a lower love. With this fall in love vibration also came the fall from grace. The search to fill this love-less void resulted in corruption, and to this very day all fears are born from this lack of love: dis-ease, dis-harmony, all from the dis-allowing of the higher love.

Open yourself up to the greatness that you are by being love in all that you . . .

. . . Think, Say & Do . . .

This is natural to you!

Remember now to remember how . . .

**The more that I love the more that I live
And so, the more I have to give . . .**

Into the love I am.

Into the love I go, thinking loving thoughts I now sow a grand new reality, free of all poverty, pain, and disease.

*P*eace, joy, and unity create this magnificent community.

*W*here we each contribute, we care and share, abundance exists everywhere.

*G*ratitude *is the natural attitude* common to all.

*W*ell-being is the only seen, in fact everything has a gracious glow about it, with a new depth of beauty. All revealed, nothing concealed. Blissfulness, magic wonderment, Heaven sent.

*E*verything hums; this comes from being in such a high state of love.

*S*uch magnitudes of much magnificence. All-encompassing Love. Grace.

*E*xpansive state of Being.
I am that I am
Into the love I return.
Divine love I am home,
Whole Being once more, a unique expression of the One.
Into the love I go . . .

Aim to better understand your thoughts

- your self
- your life

Make love your priority, in your thoughts

- your self
- your life.

Aim to love a little more each and every day.
And Heaven on Earth is here to stay . . .

Self Realization: putting Love into motion is the notion: Self Realization

Self Actualization
There are no mistakes
The things that I do
The choices that I make help to evolve me . . .

When I am being true to my authentic self
In all that I think, say and do

Unconditional love streams through me . . .

*S*elf Realization

*O*pening, Awakening, Expanding continuously into this truly unlimited Being.

*B*lissful, Peaceful, Knowing and wise, with eyes that see.

*H*eaven on Earth has arrived for me.

*C*onscious awakening, expansion of the heart. Into the truth, ears that hear.

*T*olerance and patience, the way is clear.

*L*ove, Compassion, Gratitude: healthy, happy attitude with yourself and all others, fulfilment and clarity of purpose.

*A*utonomy, Integrity, Benevolence.

*B*alance in all of one's existence.

Interconnected with all other life near and far away,

Minute through to enormous. All in One and One in All.

All life does decay in the physical, that is to say . . .

While the spiritual, mental essence returns from whence it came.

Each of us is a unique piece of the great universal consciousness.

Life's experiences can be fun, demanding, challenging while on the run. One in All and All in One.

Personal choice, freewill determines your outcome.

Attitude will see you through, depending on your point of view.

With a little focus and pure intent, good things will flow to you, Heaven sent.

So, let love guide the things you choose to think, say, and do.

To your own self be true.

Open now to your All-ness, your Wholeness, your Entirety.

Remember who you are. YOU ARE . . . YOU ARE . . . YOU ARE.

Self-realization. Remember, that unique, vibrant power house of untapped potential that awaits your activation.

Remember you're a star – A STAR . . . A STAR . . . A STAR.

What is your intent to be?

Through self-realization it is plain to see.

LOVING DREAMING

I could write about love
My whole life through,
And perhaps that's what I'll do.
But for now this short, sweet poem
Of love I write with love
To You.

May nothing but sweet love
Fill the things that you

. . . Think, Say & Do . . .

And with this,
May all of your dreams come true

Wa-Hoo!

To live fully,

Is to Love fully.

In all of your entirety,

There is no more

One can strive for or to be . . .

What is Love?

The foundation of all life is Love, therefore, it is fair to say that all life exists because of Love.

Love is an ever present, unlimited, expansive energy that is vital to all life.

Love is continually expanding through growth-life experiences: (Heinz: expand and become the greater of whom you are . . . because in essence we are all Divine love source energy.)

Love is not something to seek, earn or achieve as such. Love just is, radiating in all directions endlessly, unconditionally. Simply put, it is up to you to choose love.

Yes! Love is a choice – you choose to love and to be loved . . .

First and foremost; Love yourself and do the best you can every day.

Aim to live a little more love each day in all that you Think, Say & Do, in all ways remain true to yourself. This will allow great love to shine through into your thoughts, words and actions, as well as having a positively loving effect on all those around you.

*W*a-hooo! Allowing sweet love . . . through any of the many attributes, like kind words or a smile, offering a caring deed a helping hand when most in need.

*T*hat nod of appreciation, your true intentions, when from the heart will start an avalanche of love into motion in, through and around you, shining through all that you Think, Say & Do.

*N*ote: if you are not totally loving yourself this will come across as phony to the recipient.

*T*he easy fix: learn to love yourself better.

*Y*our intention to do so is all that is required to get this love flowing. Your intention is the invitation for love to flow into areas of your life that have been running on empty . . .

*I*t is not about being perfect or taking certain steps or following given procedures.

*I*t is about patient, consistent caring with yourself first.

*R*emember, it is your intention that counts.

SOAK in your inner pool of unconditional love and allow all false teachings, beliefs, ideals and ideas to now be lovingly replaced with your ever-present Divine truth.

You feel this truth in your heart. Deep within every man, woman and child, Divine love lives, and it is here that all is known.

What is your intention to be?

Will you act on this?

Or instead will you fear this?

Fear Not: as what is fear, none other than (False Energy Appearing Real), the illusion of the lower self. Or manmade . . .

Know now that all is forgiven, what so ever you may have done in the past was done from misaligned, misunderstood love.

Forgive yourself and others, and honor this love that resides within you . . .

*B*e You—stay true, Allow this love to now shine through, in all that you think, Say and Do.

*L*ove evolves you into the greater you, into the greater of that which you are.

*Y*our intention is all that is required. Purity of your intent – remember this must be heart sent. Say to yourself (from the heart).

Eg.:, "I now intend on being all that I can be moment by moment, day by day, my highest love expression shines through me. Always, in all ways" . . .

*A*nd every day even if in the smallest of ways, make time to laugh and play, create. These are rapid ways in which love shines through . . . resulting in a whole lot of . . .

*W*a Hoos!

*M*agic—*M*agnificence—*M*astery—through conscious effort and continuous practice.

tart your day with love.

pend your day in love.

nd your day in love, with love . . .

aking Love Your Priority.

t is with Great Love that I write these words to You!

ogether lets create a dream come true planet of Love here on Earth.

he potentials for this are right here right now.

a Hooo! Nothing but sweet love shining through . . .

bundance of Sweet Love Peace and Joy to All for All.

ith Great love,

imaya.

And so it is now so . . . I live what I believe and I believe in the Power of Love

I believe that Love is the Answer for All

That Love indeed answers a call coming from deep within us all

The Earth is shaking

The Earth is waking

Ours souls are knowing, the time is now

Love is how . . .

ACKNOWLEDGMENTS

To Lynne Ralph & Janeen Walker
Heart filled Thanks & Gratitude
For seeing as you see, doing as you do
The world is so much sweeter, Thanks to YOU!

To Pete,
For your Integrity, Devotion, Love & Support.
The natural way in which you live & give from your heart.
For all the Fun and Love you bring to me & out in me, I am ever Thankful & Grateful.

Also written by Kimaya

- Medicine in Motion
- All The Flavours Of Love
- M In M For Kids

Website: www.Kimaya.co.nz

ABOUT THE AUTHOR

New Zealand author *Kimaya* as a child inspired others through the telling of stories. Today her books convey incredible love, healing, and knowledge, gently guiding the readers, teens and adults, back to their authentic magnificence, to live a life of limitless love as she does, a true ambassador of love.

ABOUT THE BOOK

"Kimaya has a true gift! She is able to beautifully express high Universal truth and the vibration of love in a way that is simple, beautiful, and accessible to all ages and levels. When you hold her books in your hands, you can feel the love and wisdom channeling through them, and each page is pure delight. But the real gift is her radiant presence and the way she lights up the hearts of all who cross her path. She is a master soul with a message for all of us."

Adrienne Goff, USA
Author